EXPERIENCING GOD'S PRESENCE

JESUS CALLING BIBLE STUDY SERIES

EXPERIENCING GOD'S PRESENCE

EIGHT SESSIONS

Sarah Young

with Karen Lee-Thorp

THOMAS NELSON
Since 1798

NASHVILLE   MEXICO CITY   RIO DE JANEIRO

Published in Nashville, Tennessee, by Nelson Books, an imprint of Thomas Nelson. Nelson Books and Thomas Nelson are registered trademarks of HarperCollins Christian Publishing, Inc.

All Scripture quotations, unless otherwise indicated, are taken from The Holy Bible, *New International Version*®, niv®. Copyright © 1973, 1978, 1984, 2011 by Biblica, Inc.® Used by permission. All rights reserved worldwide.

Scripture quotations marked esv are taken from *The Holy Bible, English Standard Version,* copyright © 2001 by Crossway Bibles, a division of Good News Publishers. Used by permission. All rights reserved.

ISBN 978-0-7180-3586-0
ISBN 978-1-4041-0508-9 (custom)

Second Printing November 2015 / Printed in China

CONTENTS

INTRODUCTION

Sometimes our busy and difficult lives give us the impression that God is silent. We cry out to Him, but our feelings tell us that He isn't answering our prayers. In this, our feelings are incorrect. God hears our prayers and speaks right into the situations in which we find ourselves. The trouble is that our lives are often too hectic, our minds too distracted, for us to take in what God offers.

This *Jesus Calling* Bible study is designed to help individuals and groups meditate on the words of Scripture and hear them not just as words said to people long ago but as words said to us today in the here and now. The goal is to help the heart hear and respond to what the mind reads—to encounter the living God as He speaks through the Scriptures. The writer to the Hebrews tells us:

In the past God spoke to our ancestors through the prophets at many times and in various ways, but in these last days he has spoken to us by his Son, whom he appointed heir of all things, and through whom also he made the universe. The Son is the radiance of God's glory and the exact representation of his being, sustaining all things by his powerful word.

—HEBREWS 1:1–3

God has spoken to us through His Son, Jesus Christ. The New Testament gives us the chance to walk with Jesus, see what He does, and hear Him speak into the sometimes confusing situations in which we find ourselves. The Old Testament tells us the story of how God prepared a people to be the family of Jesus, and in the experiences of those men and women we find our own lives mirrored.

THE GOAL OF THIS SERIES

The *Jesus Calling Bible Study Series* offers you a chance to lay down your cares, enter God's Presence, and hear Him speak through His Word. You will get to take some time in silence studying a passage of scripture, and then if you're meeting with a group, share your insights and hear what others discovered. You'll also get to discuss excerpts from the *Jesus Calling* devotional that relate to the themes of the Bible passages. In this way, you will learn how to better make space in your life for the Spirit of God to speak to you through the Word of God and the people of God.

THE FLOW OF EACH SESSION

Each session of this study guide contains the following elements:

- CONSIDER IT. The one or two questions in this opening section serve as an icebreaker to help you start to think about the theme of the session. These questions will help you connect the theme to your own past or present experience and will help you get to know the others in your group more deeply. If you've had a busy day and your mind is full of distractions, this section will help you better focus.

- EXPERIENCE IT. Here you will find two readings from *Jesus Calling,* along with some questions for reflection. This is your chance to talk with others about the biblical principles found within the *Jesus Calling* devotions. Can you relate to what the reading describes?

- STUDY IT. Next, you'll explore one or two Scripture passages connected to the session topic and the readings from *Jesus Calling.* You will not only analyze these passages but also pray through them in ways designed to engage your heart as well as your head. The main passage is always a story in which a person encounters the Presence of God. You will pray and then spend several minutes in silence imagining what it was like to be there with the Father or Jesus in that moment. If you're meeting with a group, you will then talk about what you learned and how the passage is relevant to your life.

- LIVE IT. Finally, you will find five days' worth of suggested Scripture passages that you can pray through on your own during the week. Suggested questions for additional study and reflection are provided.

During the *Study It* portion, you will want to make notes of what comes to mind when you imagine the scene in the Scripture passage. Be sure to bring a pen to record your thoughts. The Bible passage itself is provided for you in this study guide.

FOR LEADERS

If you are leading a group through this study guide, please see the Leader's Notes at the end of the guide. You'll find background on the design of the study as well as suggested answers for some of the study questions.

GOD'S PRESENCE
INVITES YOU

1

CONSIDER IT

God is present with you. Right now. Do you believe that? Do you believe it in theory, or do you experience God's Presence as you go through your day?

God yearns to spend quiet moments with you and help you grow more and more aware of His Presence as you seek Him. In this first session, we'll begin to develop the habit of sitting in God's Presence, hearing His voice as He speaks through the Scriptures.

1. *Have you ever experienced God's Presence? If so, what did you (or what do you) experience? If you never have, do you believe God wants you to experience His Presence when you read the Scriptures? Why or why not?*

2. *What draws you to this exploration of God's Presence?*

EXPERIENCE IT

"Come to Me with a teachable spirit, eager to be changed. A close walk with Me is a life of continual newness. Do not cling to old ways as you step into a new year. Instead, seek My Face with an open mind, knowing that your journey with Me involves being *transformed by the renewing of your mind*. As you focus your thoughts on Me, be aware that I am fully attentive to you. I see you with a steady eye because my attention span is infinite. I know and understand you completely; My thoughts embrace you in everlasting Love. *I also know the plans I have for you: plans to prosper you and not to harm you, plans to give you hope and a future.* Give yourself fully to this adventure of increasing attentiveness to My Presence."

—FROM *JESUS CALLING*, JANUARY 1

3. *How eager are you to be changed? What makes you long for transformation?*

4. *What, if anything, makes you uncomfortable with change?*

5. *How do you respond to the thought that God is fully attentive to His children? Do you want that attention? Is it scary to you at all? Why or why not?*

"Relax in My healing Presence. As you spend time with Me, your thoughts tend to jump ahead to today's plans and problems. Bring your mind back to Me for refreshment and renewal. Let the Light of My Presence soak into you as you focus your thoughts on Me. Thus I equip you to face whatever the day brings. This sacrifice of time pleases Me and strengthens you. Do not skimp on our time together. Resist the clamor of tasks waiting to be done. *You have chosen what is better, and it will not be taken away from you.*"

—FROM *JESUS CALLING*, JANUARY 2

6. *What are some reasons this reflection offers for spending time in God's Presence? What are some others that come to mind?*

7. *Listening to what God is saying to you in the Scriptures is a skill that you can develop with practice. But unlike many skills, it doesn't come by trying* **harder** *but by trying* **softer**—*by relaxing and just allowing God to speak to you through the Holy Spirit. It also comes from having a right understanding of how the Lord sees you. How do you believe Jesus looks at you right now? Is He frustrated, frowning? Is He delighted with you?*

8. *In Romans 12:2, Paul writes, "Do not conform to the pattern of this world, but be transformed by the renewing of your mind." What do you think "the renewing of your mind" means?*

STUDY IT

In this section, you will reflect on a Bible passage in which Jesus visits the home of Mary and Martha. As you read, it is important to keep in mind that Jesus was close friends with these two sisters, as He was with their brother, Lazarus. Also notice that it was Martha who opened their home to Jesus. In the culture of that time, she would have been expected to provide hospitality to her guests, and she would have expected her sister to help her with the preparations.

9. *Read the following passage aloud. Then spend several minutes in silence rereading the passage and picturing yourself in the scene. You can put yourself in the place of one of the characters—Mary, Martha, one of the male disciples accompanying Jesus—or you can be in the room watching.*

> As Jesus and his disciples were on their way, he came to a village where a woman named Martha opened her home to him. She had a sister called Mary, who sat at the Lord's feet listening to what he said. But Martha was distracted by all the preparations that had to be made. She came to him and asked, "Lord, don't you care that my sister has left me to do the work by myself? Tell her to help me!"
>
> "Martha, Martha," the Lord answered, "you are worried and upset about many things, but few things are needed—or indeed only one. Mary has chosen what is better, and it will not be taken away from her."
>
> —Luke 10:38–42

Ask God to show you what He wants you to see in the passage. Use your senses to imagine the scene. What do you see? Hear? Smell? Does Jesus look at you? Say anything to you? What do you feel when He speaks to each person? What are His tone of voice and facial expressions when He speaks? Write some notes about what you have recognized through this exercise.

10. *When you sat in silence with this Scripture passage, how easy was it for you to relax in Jesus' Presence? Where did your mind go?*

11. *If you're meeting with a group, share your experience. Where did you put yourself in the story? What insights did you have? How was this like or unlike the way you usually approach the Bible?*

12. *What might Jesus be impressing on your heart through this Scripture passage?*

13. *If you're meeting with a group, how can the members pray for you? If you're using this study on your own, what would you like to say to God right now?*

LIVE IT

At the end of each session you'll find suggested Scripture readings for spending time alone with God during five days of the coming week. Each day will deal with this week's theme of God's Presence with those who are teachable, like Mary of Bethany. Read the passage slowly, pausing to think about what is being said. Rather than approaching this as an assignment to complete, think of it as an opportunity to meet with a Person. Use any of the questions that are helpful.

Day 1

Read Joshua 1:5–9. Reread it aloud and put yourself into the scene. God has just given Joshua a new and difficult task. What expression is on Joshua's face as God speaks?

With what tone of voice does God speak? What does He say?

How do these words affect Joshua?

How do you respond as you hear God say this to him? How teachable are you in this moment? Write down whatever seems significant for you to remember.

Day 2

Read Isaiah 30:20–22. The word "teachers" in verse 20 can be translated as "Teacher" (ESV), the supreme Teacher. Has God given you the bread of adversity? If so, how is this passage reassuring?

*Why do you think the voice is **behind** the one who yearns to do God's will? How will hearing this voice affect what you do?*

Are there any idols that you need to throw away? How will you ask God to help you hear His voice of guidance?

Day 3

Read Psalm 25:4–5 several times. What does the psalmist ask God to do?

Why do you suppose this is a good thing to pray for?

What does being teachable have to do with experiencing God's Presence? What would it take for your hope to be in the Lord all day long?

Expand the psalmist's prayer into your own prayer. What do you ask for?

Day 4

Read Isaiah 50:4–9. What do you think a "well-instructed tongue" (verse 4) means?

What posture does this well-instructed servant of the Lord have toward God? What attitudes does he have toward hostile people?

Do you ever have to deal with people who condemn you—or even a voice you hear in your head? How could taking this servant's posture help you with those condemning voices?

What does this passage move you to ask from God?

Day 5

Read Psalm 31:19–20 several times. What promise is given?

What do you think it means to be hidden in God's Presence? How do you suppose that works?

_____

_____

_____

_____

What does this passage move you to say to God?

_____

_____

_____

_____

GOD'S PRESENCE RESTORES YOU

CONSIDER IT

As much as we want to experience God's Presence, we often shy away from Him. We know we're unworthy in and of ourselves to approach Him. His Presence reminds us of our smallness and sinfulness.

If we have put our faith in Christ, though, we are clothed in His worthiness. Because Jesus died for us, we don't have to try to be good enough—His goodness is all we will ever need. Reminding ourselves of that will help us to stop running away from God and draw closer to Him.

In this session, we'll address this common barrier that often keeps us from seeking God's Presence.

1. *When you were a child, how important was it to the adults around you that you perform well? How did they let you know that?*

_____

_____

_____

_____

2. *On a scale of 1 to 5, how aware are you of your sinfulness most of the time?*

1	2	3	4	5
Not at all aware				Deeply aware

How aware are you of your sinfulness when you sit down to pray?

1	2	3	4	5
Not at all aware				Deeply aware

EXPERIENCE IT

"Come to Me for understanding since I know you far better than you know yourself. I comprehend you in all of your complexity; no detail of your life is hidden from Me. I view you through eyes of grace, so don't be afraid of My intimate awareness. Allow the Light of my Healing Presence to shine into the deepest recesses of your being—cleansing, healing, refreshing, and renewing you. Trust Me enough to accept the full forgiveness that I offer you continually. This great gift, which cost Me My Life, is yours for all eternity. Forgiveness is at the very core of My abiding Presence. I will never leave you or forsake you.

"When no one else seems to understand you, simply draw closer to Me. Rejoice in the One who understands you completely and loves you perfectly. As I fill you with My Love, you become a reservoir of love, overflowing into the lives of other people."

—FROM *JESUS CALLING*, MARCH 17

3. *How do you think God views you? The Bible says His thoughts are far above and beyond our thoughts (see Isaiah 55:9), but what thoughts do you tend to imagine He has about you?*

4. *What helps you believe that forgiveness is at the core of God's Presence? What gets in the way?*

5. *Have you received God's forgiveness for your sins? Why or why not?*

"I am pleased with you, My child. Allow yourself to become fully aware of My pleasure shining upon you. You don't have to perform well in order to receive My Love. In fact, a performance focus will pull you away from Me, toward some sort of Pharisaism. This can be a subtle form of idolatry: worshiping your own good works. It can also be a source of deep discouragement when your works don't measure up to your expectations.

"Shift your focus from your performance to My radiant Presence. The Light of My Love shines on you continually, regardless of your feelings or behavior. Your responsibility is to be receptive to this unconditional Love. Thankfulness and trust are your primary receptors. Thank Me for everything; trust in Me at all times. These simple disciplines will keep you open to My loving Presence."

—FROM *JESUS CALLING*, NOVEMBER 20

6. *What tends to be your stance toward God when you feel you aren't living up to His standards? Do you move toward Him or away? Why?*

7. *What helps you focus on God's Presence rather than on your performance? Or what might help you?*

STUDY IT

In this section, you'll reflect on a Bible passage in which fishing plays a prominent role. Before you read, it's helpful to know that fishing in the Lake of Gennesaret (the Sea of Galilee) was normally done at night. In the morning, the nets were carefully washed to remove debris, which was a time-consuming process. This account takes place when Simon (Peter) has already spent some time with Jesus but doesn't yet know Him well.

8. *Read the following passage aloud. Then spend several minutes in silence rereading the passage and picturing yourself in the scene (The group leader will need to keep track of time). Put yourself in the place of any character—Simon, one of the other fishermen, or even a person watching in a nearby boat.*

One day as Jesus was standing by the Lake of Gennesaret, the people were crowding around him and listening to the word of God. He saw at the water's edge two boats, left there by the fishermen, who were washing their nets. He got into one of the boats, the one belonging to Simon, and asked him to put out a little from shore. Then he sat down and taught the people from the boat.

When he had finished speaking, he said to Simon, "Put out into deep water, and let down the nets for a catch."

Simon answered, "Master, we've worked hard all night and haven't caught anything. But because you say so, I will let down the nets."

When they had done so, they caught such a large number of fish that their nets began to break. So they signaled their partners in the other boat to come and help them, and they came and filled both boats so full that they began to sink.

When Simon Peter saw this, he fell at Jesus' knees and said, "Go away from me, Lord; I am a sinful man!" For he and all his companions were astonished at the catch of fish they had taken, and so were James and John, the sons of Zebedee, Simon's partners.

Then Jesus said to Simon, "Don't be afraid; from now on you will fish for people." So they pulled their boats up on shore, left everything and followed him.

—LUKE 5:1–11

Pray for God to show you the scene, and use your senses to imagine it. What do you see? Hear? Smell? Does Jesus look at you? Say anything to you? What do you feel when He speaks to Simon? What are His tone of voice and facial expressions when He speaks? What do you feel when Simon speaks? Write some notes about what you have recognized through this exercise.

9. *If you're meeting with a group, share your experience. Where did you put yourself in the story? What insights did you have?*

10. *Why did Simon say, "Go away from me, Lord; I am a sinful man"? How typical do you think Simon's response was to others who experienced Jesus' Presence? Explain your answer.*

11. *Notice that Jesus didn't say, "No, Simon, you're not sinful." What seems to have been His attitude toward Simon's sinfulness?*

12. *What might Jesus be saying to you through this Scripture passage?*

13. *If you're meeting with a group, how can the members pray for you? If you're using this study on your own, what would you like to say to God right now?*

LIVE IT

The theme of this week's readings is entering God's Presence as a forgiven person. If you have placed your faith in Christ and are committed to following Him, your sins are forgiven. Each day, read the passage slowly, pausing to think about what is being said. Remember that this is an opportunity to meet with a Person. Use any of the questions that are helpful.

Day 1

Read Psalm 139:1–6. Pray this passage aloud slowly. What does the Lord know about you?

Are you glad that He knows you this intimately, or is it a little intimidating? Why?

Read the passage again and choose a line, a phrase, or just a word that jumps out at you. What is it about that line or word that touches you? How will you respond?

Day 2

Read Psalm 139:7–12. What is it like for you to be in Jesus' intimate Presence today? Do you rush toward Him or try to flee from Him?

Are you glad there's nowhere to go where He isn't present, or do you wish there was such a place somewhere? Why?

How easy is it for you to believe He's there with you?

What line, phrase, or word from the passage jumps out at you? What is that line or word saying to you?

Day 3

Read Ephesians 2:8–10 several times. Read this passage again and look for the words **grace,** **faith,** *and* **works** *(used twice). What role does grace play in your life?*

What role does faith play?

What role do good works play?

What role should each of these things play?

Say or write a prayer to God, telling Him what you're thinking about grace, faith, and works.

Day 4

Read Romans 5:1–5 twice. Close your eyes and picture yourself having access by faith into this grace in which every believer stands. Imagine grace as a throne room, and you're standing there with complete access. Where is Jesus in this picture?

Where is God the Father?

How far away are they from you? Is it hard for you to remain there? Why or why not?

What would you like to say to them?

Day 5

Read Luke 5:12–13. Read it again, imagining yourself either as the leper or as someone watching the scene. What do you see? Hear? Smell?

What sensations of touch do you have? What do you feel when the leper falls on the ground and begs? When Jesus touches him?

What do you take away from this experience of Jesus' Presence?

GOD'S PRESENCE
STRENGTHENS YOU

Consider It

There are times in our lives when we are desperate for God's Presence. Overwhelming circumstances become bearable when we know we're not alone but are being cared for by a God who sees us and loves us. Sometimes, though, those very circumstances tempt us to run away instead of running toward God's Presence.

In this session, we'll consider these two options of running away and running toward and try to be open to the Lord meeting us in our desperate place.

1. *In times of stress or conflict, we respond with either a* **fight** *or a* **flight** *response. Our natural bent is either to fight with the person or situation or to flee from it. Which of these comes more naturally to you: fighting or fleeing? (If neither comes naturally to you, what do you do instead?)*

Experience It

"Come to Me when you are weak and weary. Rest snugly in My everlasting arms. I do not despise your weakness, My child. Actually, it draws Me closer to you because weakness stirs up My compassion—my yearning to help. Accept yourself in your weariness, knowing that I understand how difficult your journey has been.

"Do not compare yourself with others who seem to skip along their life-paths with ease. Their journeys have been different from yours, and I have gifted them with abundant energy. I have gifted you with fragility, providing opportunities for your spirit to blossom in My Presence. Accept this gift as a sacred treasure: delicate, yet glowing with brilliant

Light. Rather than struggling to disguise or deny your weakness, allow Me to bless you richly through it."

—From *Jesus Calling*, August 12

2. *When do you most feel weak and weary? What do you usually do to deal with that problem? How well does that work?*

3. *Do you believe your weakness stirs up God's compassion? How does your belief (or lack of it) affect the way you deal with weakness?*

4. *You have been spending time with God in the Scriptures for a couple of weeks now. How has that affected you? How easy has it been? How fruitful? If it has been hard, what might help you?*

"There is no place so desolate that you cannot find Me there. When Hagar fled from her mistress, Sarah, into the wilderness, she thought she was utterly alone and forsaken. But Hagar encountered Me in that desolate place. There she addressed Me as the Living One who sees me. Through that encounter with My Presence, she gained courage to return to her mistress.

"No set of circumstances could ever isolate you from My loving Presence. Not only do I see you always; I see you as a redeemed saint, gloriously radiant in My righteousness. That is why I take great delight in you and rejoice over you with singing!"

—FROM *JESUS CALLING*, AUGUST 30

5. *Have you ever been in circumstances that seemed to isolate you from God's loving Presence? If so, what were the circumstances?*

6. *As a believer in Christ, how do you respond to the idea that God, in fact, was present with you in those circumstances? Can you believe that God was there, or was the sense of His absence too strong?*

7. *Do you see yourself as a redeemed saint, gloriously arrayed in Christ's righteousness? What helps you see yourself that way? What hinders you?*

Study It

In this section, you'll spend some time in the story of Hagar mentioned in the above excerpt from *Jesus Calling*. Hagar was the slave of Sarai (later renamed Sarah), the wife of Abraham. Sarai had been unable to have children, so she convinced Abraham to try to have a child by a method that was a custom at that time. Sarai gave her slave to Abraham in the hopes they would be able to build a family through her. Hagar did get pregnant, but then she became insolent toward Sarai about it, and Sarai in turn became angry and envious. Sarai mistreated Hagar—which probably means she had her whipped or beaten—so Hagar ran away into the desert. Here the Lord found her in a desperate state.

8. *Read the following passage aloud. Then spend several minutes in silence rereading the passage and picturing yourself in the scene (The group leader will need to keep track of time). You can put yourself in the place of Hagar or watch the scene from nearby.*

> The angel of the LORD found Hagar near a spring in the desert; it was the spring that is beside the road to Shur. And he said, "Hagar, slave of Sarai, where have you come from, and where are you going?"
>
> "I'm running away from my mistress Sarai," she answered.
>
> Then the angel of the LORD told her, "Go back to your mistress and submit to her." The angel added, "I will increase your descendants so much that they will be too numerous to count."
>
> The angel of the LORD also said to her: "You are now pregnant and you will give birth to a son. You shall name him Ishmael, for the LORD has heard of your misery. He will be a wild donkey of a man; his hand will be against everyone and everyone's hand against him, and he will live in hostility toward all his brothers."
>
> She gave this name to the LORD who spoke to her: "You are the God who sees me," for she said, "I have now seen the One who sees me."
>
> —GENESIS 16:7–13

Ask God to guide you. What do you see? Hear? Feel? Are you thirsty? Is the angel visible or just a voice? What do you feel each time he speaks? What are his tone of voice and facial expressions? What do you feel as Hagar responds? What is her body language when the angel tells her to go back to Sarai? Write some notes about what you have recognized through this exercise.

---

9. *If you're meeting with a group, share your experience. Where did you put yourself in the story? What insights did you have?*

10. *In the end, Hagar knew that the Lord Himself had been present with her. Were you able to sense God's Presence in this account, or was it merely words on a page?*

11. *God sent Hagar back to the same circumstances from which she fled. How do you respond to that? Would knowing you were seen by God make the circumstances bearable, or do you think God should have given her better circumstances?*

12. *What might Jesus be saying to you through this Scripture passage?*

13. *If you're meeting with a group, how can the members pray for you? If you're using this study on your own, what would you like to say to God right now?*

Live It

The theme of this week's readings is moving toward God's Presence, especially when you're feeling desperate. Each day, read the passage slowly, pausing to think about what is being said. Remember that this is an opportunity to meet with a Person. Use any of the questions that are helpful.

Day 1

Read Romans 8:22–25 twice. Can you identify with **groaning** *as in the pains of childbirth? What circumstances make you feel that way?*

What does the passage say Christians should hope for?

How easy is it for you to hope for what you don't see?

Ask God to strengthen you with His Presence so you can wait with hope and patience.

Day 2

Read Romans 8:26–27 twice. What is a situation you don't know how to pray about?

How do you need the Holy Spirit to intercede for you in that situation?

Hold your hands out, open, and imagine yourself putting that situation into the Holy Spirit's hands. Tell Him you need Him to intercede for you. If the wordless groans come, let them come.

Day 3

Read Romans 8:28–30 twice. Do you hear verse 28 as an encouragement or as a platitude? Why?

_____

_____

_____

_____

_____

Is there an area of your life where you are finding it hard to see God working for your good or the good of someone you love? If so, what area?

_____

_____

_____

_____

_____

Ask God to use this circumstance to make you more like His Son and for Him to see you and be present with you in this situation.

Day 4

Read Romans 8:31–34 twice. What reasons do these verses offer God's people for being confident in the face of suffering?

What does this passage say about condemning voices? Why do you think condemning voices are such a big issue for Christians?

How does it help you to know that Jesus is praying for you right now?

Choose one verse from this passage and turn it into a prayer that you pray back to God.

Day 5

Read Romans 8:35–39 again. What does this passage say about God's Presence for those who believe in Him?

Are you ever tempted to feel that circumstances separate you from the love of God? What are the ways this passage reassures you that God is present with you?

Thank God today for the promises He gives believers in His Word.

GOD'S PRESENCE BRINGS YOU PEACE

CONSIDER IT

Some of us experience anxiety all through the day, regardless of what is happening. Others of us worry about particular things: money, work, children, health, an unsafe neighborhood. We may fear failure, or the unknown, or becoming ill, or losing a job. We may fear for our loved ones or ourselves. One way or another, each of us encounters fear from time to time, and we need to be confident that God is present with us in the midst of our fears. In this session we'll reflect on the idea that no matter what is happening, we can be deeply and completely safe in God's Presence.

1. *When you were a child, what were some of the things you were afraid of? How many of these fears, if any, have you carried over into adulthood?*

_____

_____

_____

_____

2. *As an adult, what is one thing you worry about or one thing that gives you a zing of fear?*

_____

_____

_____

_____

_____

EXPERIENCE IT

"Let Me prepare you for the day that stretches out before you. I know exactly what this day will contain, whereas you have only vague ideas about it. You would like to see a map, showing all the twists and turns of your journey. You'd feel more prepared if you could somehow visualize what is on the road ahead. However, there is a better way to be prepared for *whatever* you will encounter today: Spend quality time with Me.

"I will not show you what is on the road ahead, but I will thoroughly equip you for the journey. My living Presence is your Companion each step of the way. Stay in continual communication with Me, whispering My Name whenever you need to redirect your thoughts. Thus, you can walk through this day with your focus on Me. My abiding Presence is the best road map available."

—FROM *JESUS CALLING*, JANUARY 12

3. *What does "quality time" with Jesus mean for you? What obstacles tend to come between you and spending quality time with Jesus each day?*

4. *What do you think about the idea of whispering Jesus' Name throughout the day, especially during those times when you're tempted to worry or feel afraid? Does that sound like something that would make a difference for you? What makes you inclined to try it or not try it?*

"Whenever you feel distant from Me, whisper My name in loving trust. This simple prayer can restore your awareness of My Presence.

"My Name is constantly abused in the world, where people use it as a curse word. This verbal assault reaches all the way to heaven; every word is heard and recorded. When you trustingly whisper My Name, My aching ears are soothed. The grating rancor of the world's blasphemies cannot compete with a trusting child's utterance: 'Jesus.' The power of My Name to bless both you and Me is beyond your understanding."

—FROM *JESUS CALLING*, JULY 12

5. *Do you think it actually delights Jesus to hear people use His Name as a prayer? How does it affect you when you think about that?*

6. *What is the one thing you will have to overcome in order to build a habit of whispering Jesus' Name throughout the day? What will it take for you to overcome that?*

_____

_____

_____

_____

STUDY IT

In this section, you're going to read a passage in which Jesus and His followers are in a boat on the Sea of Galilee, the same lake or sea where Simon was fishing in the passage from session 2. This is a large freshwater lake in Israel, about thirteen miles long, surrounded by mountains. Violent storms sometimes sweep down from the mountains and across the lake. In Jesus' day, it was easy for such a storm to capsize a fishing boat.

7. *Read the following passage aloud. Then spend several minutes in silence rereading the passage and picturing yourself in the scene (The group leader will need to keep track of time.) You can put yourself in the place of one of the disciples or watch the scene from a nearby boat—just be sure to put yourself in the storm.*

> Then [Jesus] got into the boat and his disciples followed him. Suddenly a furious storm came up on the lake, so that the waves swept over the boat. But Jesus was sleeping. The disciples went and woke him, saying, "Lord, save us! We're going to drown!"
>
> He replied, "You of little faith, why are you so afraid?" Then he got up and rebuked the winds and the waves, and it was completely calm.
>
> The men were amazed and asked, "What kind of man is this? Even the winds and the waves obey him!"
>
> —MATTHEW 8:23–27

Ask God to guide you, and use your senses to imagine the scene. What do you see? Hear? Smell? Feel? What is the storm like? What do you feel as it builds? What tone of voice and body language do the various speakers have at each point in the story? What do you feel when the disciples speak? What do you feel when Jesus speaks? Write down some notes about what you have recognized through this exercise.

8. *If you're meeting with a group, share your experience of putting yourself into this story. What was it like to be in that boat? What insights did you have? What did you envision about Jesus' and the disciples' tone of voice and body language?*

9. *Were the disciples' fears reasonable? Why or why not?*

10. *Was it right for the disciples to wake Jesus and call upon Him to save them? Why or why not? Why did Jesus say they had "little faith"? What would great faith have looked like in this situation?*

11. *Are you in a storm? If so, what would great faith look like for you in that storm?*

12. *What might Jesus be saying to you through this Scripture passage?*

_____

_____

_____

_____

_____

_____

13. *If you're meeting with a group, how can the members pray for you? If you're using this study on your own, what would you like to say to God right now?*

_____

_____

_____

_____

_____

LIVE IT

The theme of this week's readings is finding your safety in Jesus' Presence. Each day, read the passage slowly, pausing to think about what is being said. Remember that this is an opportunity to meet with a Person. Use any of the questions that are helpful.

Day 1

Read Psalm 116:1–6 twice. What emotions does the psalmist express? Where do you see his desperation?

What role does the Name of the Lord play in the story the psalmist tells?

What do you think is involved in calling on the Name of the Lord beyond simply speaking the word? What attitudes and actions might be involved?

Try calling on the Name of the Lord now, and try whispering Jesus' Name in prayer as you go through your day.

Day 2

Read Psalm 148:1–6, 13. What reasons for praising the Name of the Lord does the psalmist give?

What reasons do you have for praising Him?

How easy is it for you to praise the Name of the Lord? What helps you?

Praise Jesus' Name now, and remember to bring His Name to your mind and lips often as you go through your day.

Day 3

Read Psalm 31:9–12. What emotions does the psalmist express? Why does he feel this way?

In what ways can you identify with the psalmist?

Read verses 1–5. What does the psalmist ask for? What are you moved to ask for?

Offer up to God any of the psalmist's words that speak for your heart's cry. Keep the Name of Jesus on your lips today.

Day 4

Read Psalm 7:1–5. What does this psalmist need to be safe from?

_____

_____

_____

_____

What is he confident the Lord will do for him?

_____

_____

_____

_____

Why does the psalmist invite the Lord to look at his actions and point out any guilt? How easy is it for you to claim guiltlessness in God's eyes?

_____

_____

_____

_____

Recall what Jesus has done for you. How does that recollection help you deal with condemning voices?

Thank the Lord that believers can seek safety in Him without guilt that would separate them from Him.

Day 5

Read Exodus 33:12–20. What role does the Lord's Presence play in this story?

Moses says to God, "Show me your glory," and the Lord replies, "I will proclaim my name, the LORD, in your presence" (verses 18–19). Why would hearing the Lord proclaim His Name be connected to seeing His glory?

What does that tell you about the importance of His Name?

_____

_____

_____

_____

Read the passage again, looking for things to pray for. Choose one thing you especially want to ask God to provide to you.

GOD'S PRESENCE
AWES YOU

CONSIDER IT

God's Presence can be extremely comforting—He comes to us gently when we are in distress. But the Lord isn't just our comfort. He is also the Lord Almighty, the Ultimate Authority, the Creator of the Universe. Entering His Presence is treading on holy ground.

In this session we will see what it's like to experience God in the splendor of His holiness. We'll start by thinking about our earthly fathers, because the way we see our earthly father influences the way we respond to our heavenly Father.

1. *What was your earthly father like when you were a small child? Was he someone you went to when you scraped your knee? Was he someone you looked up to? Did he scare you? Was he absent?*

_____

_____

_____

_____

2. *What is* **awe**? *When, if ever, have you felt awe?*

_____

_____

_____

_____

EXPERIENCE IT

"Let Me anoint you with My Presence. I am King of kings and Lord of lords, dwelling in unapproachable Light. When you draw near to Me, I respond by coming closer to you. As My Presence envelops you, you may feel overwhelmed by My Power and Glory. This is a form of worship: sensing your smallness in comparison to My Greatness.

"Man has tended to make himself the measure of all things. But man's measure is too tiny to comprehend My majestic vastness. That is why most people do not see Me at all, even though they live and move and have their being in Me.

"Enjoy the radiant beauty of My Presence. Declare My glorious Being to the world!"

—FROM *JESUS CALLING*, MAY 28

3. *When you think about being overwhelmed by God's power and glory, does that sound like a good thing? An uncomfortable thing? Why?*

4. *What does the statement, "Man has tended to make himself the measure of all things," mean to you? What is wrong with doing that?*

"Come to Me and listen! Attune yourself to My voice, and receive My richest blessings. Marvel at the wonder of communing with the Creator of the universe while sitting in the comfort of your home. Kings who reign on earth tend to make themselves inaccessible; ordinary people almost never gain an audience with them. Even dignitaries must plow through red tape and protocol in order to speak with royalty.

"Though I am King of the universe, I am totally accessible to you. I am with you wherever you are. Nothing can separate you from My Presence! When I cried out from the cross, "It is finished!" the curtain of the temple was torn in two from top to bottom. This opened the way for you to meet Me face-to-Face, with no need of protocol or priests. I, the King of kings, am your constant Companion."

—FROM *JESUS CALLING*, SEPTEMBER 26

5. *What is involved in attuning yourself to God's voice in the Scriptures?*

_____

_____

_____

_____

6. *Have you begun to experience God as your constant companion? If so, what is that like? If not, do you have any greater sense of His Presence now than you had before the study began?*

_____

_____

_____

_____

STUDY IT

In this section, you're going to read a passage from the Old Testament in which a man named Isaiah goes into the temple in Jerusalem and has a vision of God. In this vision, he also sees several seraphim, a type of angel. This is Isaiah's first-ever vision of God, and the Lord calls him to be a prophet to speak His words to Israel.

7. Read the following passage aloud. Then spend several minutes in silence rereading the passage and picturing yourself in the scene (The group leader will need to keep track of time). You can put yourself in the place of Isaiah or watch the scene from a corner of the room.

In the year that King Uzziah died, I saw the LORD, high and exalted, seated on a throne; and the train of his robe filled the temple. Above him were seraphim, each with six wings: With two wings they covered their faces, with two they covered their feet, and with two they were flying. And they were calling to one another: "Holy, holy, holy is the LORD Almighty; the whole earth is full of his glory."

At the sound of their voices the doorposts and thresholds shook and the temple was filled with smoke.

"Woe to me!" I cried. "I am ruined! For I am a man of unclean lips, and I live among a people of unclean lips, and my eyes have seen the King, the LORD Almighty."

Then one of the seraphim flew to me with a live coal in his hand, which he had taken with tongs from the altar. With it he touched my mouth and said, "See, this has touched your lips; your guilt is taken away and your sin atoned for."

Then I heard the voice of the LORD saying, "Whom shall I send? And who will go for us?"

And I said, "Here am I. Send me!"

—ISAIAH 6:1–8

Ask God to guide your understanding, and use your senses to imagine the scene. What do you see? Hear? Feel? What do the seraphim look like? Can you smell the smoke within the temple? What tone of voice and body language do the various speakers have at each point in this account? What do you feel when Isaiah speaks? What do you feel when the Lord speaks? Write some notes about what you have recognized through this excercise.

8. If you're meeting with a group, share your experience of putting yourself into this story. What was it like to be in the temple seeing the Lord like this? What insights did you have? How was Isaiah's experience like or unlike other biblical accounts of God's Presence?

9. *Why did Isaiah say, "I am ruined"? What do you think he was afraid was going to happen?*

10. *Isaiah knew that a man with "unclean lips" was unprepared to be in the Presence of the holy Lord. What do you think it means to have "unclean lips"? Why did a hot coal from the altar of sacrifice take away Isaiah's guilt?*

11. *How does Jesus' sacrifice on the cross affect the way His followers approach Him today? (Refer to the second reading under "Experience It," which reflects what God's Word says about the impact of the crucifixion in this regard.)*

12. *What might Jesus be saying to you through this Scripture passage?*

_____

_____

_____

_____

_____

13. *If you're meeting with a group, how can the members pray for you? If you're using this study on your own, what would you like to say to God right now?*

_____

_____

_____

_____

_____

LIVE IT

The theme of this week's readings is approaching God's Presence with awe. Each day, read the passage slowly, pausing to think about what is being said. Remember that this is an opportunity to meet with a Person. Use any of the questions that are helpful.

Day 1

Read Exodus 3:1–6. Imagine yourself in the scene, either as Moses or as someone watching. Picture the bush that burns without being consumed. Can you smell smoke? Can you feel the heat? What do you feel when God speaks?

What do you learn about holiness as Moses takes off his shoes?

Why is Moses afraid to look at God? How does it affect you to think that this same God invites you into His Presence?

What do you want to say to God today?

Day 2

Read Exodus 3:7–9. What do these verses add to the picture of the Lord in verses 1–6?

What does the Lord care about? How do you imagine the sound of His voice as He says these words?

How easy is it for you to conceive of a God who is both awe-inspiring and caring? Is this a God you want to draw close to? Why or why not?

What will you say to God?

Last week you practiced speaking the Name of Jesus as you went through your day. How does reading Isaiah and Exodus affect the way you speak His Name?

Day 3

Read Psalm 29:1-9. Read this psalm again and take note of each statement about the Lord. Choose one word or phrase that strikes you as especially significant. Why did you choose that one?

Why would the psalmist use thunder and lightning to describe the Lord?

What is good about serving a God like this? Is this a God you want to draw close to? Why or why not?

What will you say to the Lord?

Day 4

Read Isaiah 55:1–3 twice. What waters is Isaiah talking about? What is the wine and milk? Why does he describe it as wine and milk?

What are you thirsty for? Does the Lord's Presence satisfy what you're hungry and thirsty for?

What are the things you've labored for that don't satisfy? What would you like to do differently?

Day 5

Read Isaiah 55:6–9 twice. What does this passage tell God's people to do?

What reasons does it give for doing this? What other reasons can you think of?

What are some of God's ways that are higher than our ways?

Do you have any unrighteous ways or thoughts that you need to turn away from? If so, what are they? What will you say to God about them?

GOD'S PRESENCE
SAVES YOU

CONSIDER IT

When we lose someone or something dear to us, we grieve. Some of us grieve openly, while others of us keep it private. Many people say God feels far away when they are grieving. But Jesus is all too familiar with suffering. He knows what it's like to lose everything, and He knows what it's like to watch the people He loves endure the worst possible grief. In this session we'll explore how we can experience the Lord's Presence during times of loss and grief.

1. *Think of a time when you experienced a significant loss. This might be the loss of a loved one to death, the loss of a job, a divorce, the loss of your house, or the loss of your health. (If you've never had a really big loss, think of the biggest one you have experienced.) What did you do to cope with that loss? Did you just "pull yourself together" and move on? Did you talk to people? Did you withdraw? Did you cry a lot? Eat a lot? Explain.*

EXPERIENCE IT

"Do not expect to be treated fairly in this life. People will say and do hurtful things to you, things that you don't deserve. When someone mistreats you, try to view it as an opportunity to grow in grace. See how quickly you can forgive the one who has wounded you. Don't be concerned about setting the record straight. Instead of obsessing about other people's opinions of you, keep your focus on Me. Ultimately, it is My view of you that counts.

"As you concentrate on relating to Me, remember that I have clothed you in My righteousness and holiness. I see you attired in these radiant garments, which I bought for you with My blood. This also is not fair; it is pure gift. When others treat you unfairly, remember that My ways with you are much better than fair. My ways are Peace and Love, which I have poured out into your heart by My Spirit."

—FROM *JESUS CALLING*, OCTOBER 28

2. *What do you typically do when you are treated unfairly? How easy is it for you to forgive? Why?*

3. *What do you think about viewing mistreatment as an opportunity to grow in grace? Does that make sense to you? How hard does it sound? Why?*

4. *How often are you aware that God is treating you more than fairly? How often do you feel that God is treating you less than fairly? Why?*

"I am with you. I am with you. I am with you. Heaven's bells continually peal with that promise of My Presence. Some people never hear those bells because their minds are earthbound and their hearts are closed to Me. Others hear the bells only once or twice in their lifetimes, in rare moments of seeking Me above all else. My desire is that my "sheep" hear My voice continually, for I am the ever-present Shepherd.

"Quietness is the classroom where you learn to hear My voice. Beginners need a quiet place in order to still their minds. As you advance in this discipline, you gradually learn to carry the stillness with you wherever you go. When you step back into the mainstream of life, strain to hear those glorious bells: I am with you. I am with you. I am with you."

—FROM *JESUS CALLING*, OCTOBER 30

5. *As a Christian, what helps you hear the Lord saying, "I am with you. I am with you"? What deafens you to His nearness?*

6. *Do you make time for quietness each day? If so, how does it affect your spirit? If you find it hard to make time for quiet moments with God, how do you think that affects you?*

STUDY IT

In this section, you're going to read part of the story of Jesus' crucifixion. The soldiers have stripped Jesus to humiliate Him (nudity is extremely shameful in this culture). They have nailed Him to the cross at his wrists and ankles. Now they are dividing up his clothes. Jesus' mother, some other women, and His disciple John are watching. (John is called "the disciple whom he loved.") The other male disciples are all in hiding, afraid that they too will be arrested. Jesus' mother is a widow, and now that Jesus won't be around to make sure she has a house and food, He wants to put her in someone's care. Her other living male relatives don't believe in Jesus, so Jesus asks John to take on the job of caring for His mother.

7. *Read the following passage aloud. Then spend several minutes in silence rereading the passage and picturing yourself in the scene (The group leader will need to keep track of time). You can put yourself in the place of Jesus' mother, one of the other women, John, or another bystander.*

> When the soldiers crucified Jesus, they took his clothes, dividing them into four shares, one for each of them, with the undergarment remaining. This garment was seamless, woven in one piece from top to bottom.
>
> "Let's not tear it," they said to one another. "Let's decide by lot who will get it."

This happened that the scripture might be fulfilled that said, "They divided my clothes among them and cast lots for my garment."

So this is what the soldiers did.

Near the cross of Jesus stood his mother, his mother's sister, Mary the wife of Clopas, and Mary Magdalene. When Jesus saw his mother there, and the disciple whom he loved standing nearby, he said to her, "Woman, here is your son," and to the disciple, "Here is your mother." From that time on, this disciple took her into his home.

Later, knowing that everything had now been finished, and so that Scripture would be fulfilled, Jesus said, "I am thirsty." A jar of wine vinegar was there, so they soaked a sponge in it, put the sponge on a stalk of the hyssop plant, and lifted it to Jesus' lips. When he had received the drink, Jesus said, "It is finished." With that, he bowed his head and gave up his spirit.

—JOHN 19:23–30

Ask God to guide you, and use your senses to imagine the scene. What is it like to be up close to a crucifixion? What do the soldiers look and sound like? What are the women doing? What are the tone of voice and body language of the various speakers at each point in this account? What do you feel as the story unfolds? Write some notes about what you have recognized through this exercise.

8. *If you're meeting with a group, share your experience of putting yourself into this story. What was it like to be at the cross seeing Jesus like this? How did the women affect you? How did the soldiers affect you? How did imagining yourself with Jesus in that moment differ from what you envisioned with Isaiah in the temple?*

9. *What do you think Jesus' voice sounded like when He spoke from the cross? How would you compare that voice to the voice of the Lord speaking to Isaiah in the temple?*

10. *How would you describe what this experience may have been like for Jesus' mother? What would it take to hang onto faith in God in this situation?*

11. *Have you ever suffered deep grief? If so, what sense of God's Presence, if any, did you have at that time? If God seemed absent, what was that like?*

12. *What might Jesus be saying to you through this Scripture passage?*

13. *If you're meeting with a group, how can the members pray for you? If you're using this study on your own, what would you like to say to God right now?*

LIVE IT

The theme of this week's readings is being in God's Presence at a moment of deep grief. Each day, read the passage slowly, pausing to think about what is being said. Remember that this is an opportunity to meet with a Person. Use any of the questions that are helpful.

Day 1

Read Luke 23:32–43. Put yourself in the scene as you have been learning to do. You can be anyone in the story other than Jesus. What do you see? Hear? Feel?

Is it hard for you to go back to the cross yet again? Why or why not?

In what ways is Jesus' Presence here comforting? In what ways is it not comforting?

What do you find yourself wanting to do in response to this scene?

Day 2

Read Luke 23:32–43 again. This time, focus on the themes of forgiveness and fairness. Why does Jesus forgive the people who are crucifying Him?

Look at what the second criminal says about getting what he deserves (see verses 40–42). Does he deserve forgiveness? Does he get it?

Would you rather receive justice or mercy? Would you rather give others justice or mercy?

Jesus is merciful even in His moment of greatest loss. How does loss affect your ability to forgive others?

Day 3

Read Luke 23:48–56. Put yourself into the scene as Joseph or one of the women watching him. How does Joseph handle the dead body of Jesus? Why does he do this?

What would it feel like to handle Jesus' dead body in this way? What might Joseph be thinking and feeling?

What might Jesus' mother be thinking? Why do they care about the body when Jesus' spirit is gone?

Where is the Presence of God at this moment when Jesus is dead? If you've lost a loved one, how does this scene affect you?

85

Day 4

Read Psalm 22:1–5. How would you describe the psalmist's emotions? What is his attitude toward God?

Read the passage again and look for any words that speak to your current situation. Which words did you choose? Why did you choose those?

If you are in a completely different place than this, how is your situation different? How grateful are you that it's different?

How easy is it for you to be this honest with God? Tell God whatever this psalm moves you to say.

_____

_____

_____

_____

Day 5

Read Psalm 22:1, 25–31. Jesus quoted the first line of this psalm when He hung on the cross (see Mark 15:34). In the culture of the time, quoting the first line was a way of referring to the whole psalm. Why was this an appropriate psalm for Jesus to be thinking of on the cross?

_____

_____

_____

_____

How is the statement, "He has done it!" (verse 31), appropriate for Jesus' situation?

_____

_____

_____

_____

What might Jesus' mother and the other women have thought when they heard Him refer to this psalm? What would those words mean to Jesus' mother?

_____

_____

_____

_____

How does it affect you to think of Jesus in connection with this psalm? (You can read the whole psalm and think about how it relates to Jesus' experience.)

_____

_____

_____

_____

GOD'S PRESENCE
GIVES YOU JOY

CONSIDER IT

Sometimes it feels as if our grief will never end. When a loved one has died, we feel the deep loss of knowing that we will never see that person again on this earth. We can feel similar hopelessness about a persistent health problem, a relationship difficulty, or the loss of a job. God feels absent.

On one remarkable morning in history, however, someone who was dead stopped being dead. That morning changed history forever. It conquered the unconquerable and restored Jesus' Presence to us. In this session, we'll go to that remarkable morning and consider how it changes everything for us, no matter what seemingly unconquerable difficulty troubles us.

1. *Has your awareness of God's Presence changed in any way since the beginning of this study? If so, how? If not, how close or distant does Jesus seem to you right now? Has spending time alone with Him during the week affected that?*

2. *Have you continued to whisper Jesus' Name in prayer as you go through your day? If so, how has that made a difference?*

EXPERIENCE IT

"I am with you and for you. When you decide on a course of action that is in line with My will, nothing in heaven or on earth can stop you. You may encounter many obstacles as you move toward your goal, but don't be discouraged—never give up! With My help, you can overcome any obstacle. Do not expect an easy path as you journey hand in hand with Me, but do remember that I, your very-present Helper, am omnipotent.

"Much, much stress results from your wanting to make things happen before their times have come. One of the main ways I assert My sovereignty is in the timing of events. If you want to stay close to Me and do things My way, ask Me to show you the path forward moment by moment. Instead of dashing headlong toward your goal, let Me set the pace. Slow down, and enjoy the journey in My Presence."

—FROM *JESUS CALLING*, JANUARY 9

3. *Do you ever experience stress from wanting to make something happen before its time has come? If so, when have you done that? If not, what helps you avoid doing that?*

4. *How do you think your life would be different if you always asked Jesus to show you the path forward moment by moment?*

"I am all around you, hovering over you even as you seek My Face. I am nearer than you dare believe, closer than the air you breathe. If My children could only recognize My Presence, they would never feel lonely again. *I know every thought before you think it, every word before you speak it.* My Presence impinges on your innermost being. Can you see the absurdity of trying to hide anything from Me? You can easily deceive other people, and even yourself; but I read you like an open, large-print book.

"Deep within themselves, most people have some awareness of My imminent Presence. Many people run from Me and vehemently deny My existence, because My closeness terrifies them. But My own children have nothing to fear, for I have cleansed them by My blood and clothed them in My righteousness. Be blessed by My intimate nearness. Since I live in you, let Me also live through you, shining My Light into the darkness.

—FROM *JESUS CALLING*, AUGUST 24

5. *Why might Jesus' closeness terrify a person?*

6. *How does it affect you to contemplate the fact that Jesus knows your every thought before you think it? Does that comfort you? Scare you? Why?*

STUDY IT

In this section, you'll read what Mary Magdalene saw early on Sunday morning after Jesus' crucifixion. Mary was one of Jesus' female followers for much of His ministry. He drove seven demons out of her, and in gratitude she supported His ministry financially (see Luke 8:1–3). She was one of the women who witnessed His crucifixion. She went to His tomb at dawn to finish the burial rites (see Luke 24:1) but found the tomb empty and assumed that someone had taken the body (see John 20:1–2). After reporting the missing body to the disciples, she returned to the empty tomb to grieve.

7. *Read the following passage aloud. Then spend several minutes in silence rereading the passage and picturing yourself in the scene (The group leader will need to keep track of time.) You can put yourself in the place of Mary Magdalene or a bystander.*

Now Mary stood outside the tomb crying. As she wept, she bent over to look into the tomb and saw two angels in white, seated where Jesus' body had been, one at the head and the other at the foot.

They asked her, "Woman, why are you crying?"

"They have taken my Lord away," she said, "and I don't know where they have put him." At this, she turned around and saw Jesus standing there, but she did not realize that it was Jesus.

He asked her, "Woman, why are you crying? Who is it you are looking for?"

Thinking he was the gardener, she said, "Sir, if you have carried him away, tell me where you have put him, and I will get him."

Jesus said to her, "Mary."

She turned toward him and cried out in Aramaic, "Rabboni!" (which means "Teacher").

Jesus said, "Do not hold on to me, for I have not yet ascended to the Father. Go instead to my brothers and tell them, 'I am ascending to my Father and your Father, to my God and your God.'"

Mary Magdalene went to the disciples with the news: "I have seen the Lord!" And she told them that he had said these things to her.

—JOHN 20:11–18

Ask God to guide your understanding, and use your senses to imagine the scene. What is Mary's body language at each point in the action? What tone of voice do the characters use? What do you feel as the story unfolds as the dawn turns into day? Write down some notes about what you have recognized through this exercise.

8. *If you're meeting with a group, share your experience of putting yourself into this story. What was it like to imagine yourself with Jesus like this after spending last week at the cross with Him? How did it affect you when Jesus spoke Mary's name?*

9. *Why do you think Mary didn't recognize Jesus at first?*

10. *Because Jesus says, "Do not hold on to me," we know that Mary must have taken His hands or thrown herself at his feet. Why did she do this? What was she expressing? What tone of voice do you think Jesus used with Mary when He told her not to cling to Him?*

11. *Would it be hard for you not to try to hold on to an experience of Jesus' Presence like this? Why or why not? Why would Jesus say, "Do not hold on to me . . . Go instead to my brothers"?*

12. *What might Jesus be saying to you through this Scripture passage?*

13. *If you're meeting with a group, how can the members pray for you? If you're using this study on your own, what would you like to say to God right now?*

LIVE IT

The theme of this week's readings is experiencing the exhilarating Presence of the resurrected Jesus, the Son of God. Each day, read the passage slowly, pausing to think about what is being said. Remember that this is an opportunity to meet with a Person. Use any of the questions that are helpful.

Day 1

Read Luke 24:13–27. Put yourself into the scene as one of the two disciples. What do you see? Hear?

What tone of voice does Cleopas use? What is his body language?

What about Jesus? What do you feel when He says the disciples are foolish? Can you identify with the disciples in any way?

Why do you think Jesus doesn't make Himself known immediately? Why does He make Himself known by explaining the Old Testament Scriptures?

How does this moment of Jesus' Presence affect you?

Day 2

Read Luke 24:28–45. Also read Luke 22:19, a verse from Luke's account of Jesus' last meal with His disciples before His crucifixion. Why do you think Jesus makes Himself known to the two disciples in that moment of taking bread, blessing it, breaking it, and giving it?

How does Jesus later make Himself known to the other disciples in Jerusalem?

How does Jesus make Himself known in your life?

Thank Him today for the ways He does this.

Day 3

Read Luke 24:36–44. Put yourself in the scene. What do you see? Hear? What is it like to touch Jesus, even His wounds?

What do you feel as the scene unfolds?

What does joy look like on someone's face? What does it feel like?

Are you able to enter into the disciples' joy and amazement? Why or why not?

Talk to Jesus about your experience with this scene.

Day 4

Read Luke 24:45–48. How does Jesus summarize the gospel message?

What does "repentance for the forgiveness of sins" mean? How do Jesus' words affect you?

Are you a witness of these things? What does it mean to be a witness? What are the implications of that?

Does being a witness feel like something heavy expected of you or like something you want to be? Why is that?

Day 5

Read John 20:24–29. Put yourself into the scene. What do you see? Hear? Feel?

Do you need what Thomas needs? Why doesn't the Lord give us all the opportunity He gives to Thomas?

Are you able to believe without seeing? How does the lack of seeing affect your faith in Jesus' Presence? Tell Jesus honestly where you are on this.

GOD'S PRESENCE
EMPOWERS YOU

Consider It

Jesus was bodily present on earth for thirty-three years, and His disciples spent more than three years with Him. That time came to an end at last, though, and then the disciples had to start trusting in His Presence without seeing Him bodily. That is the situation in which we find ourselves as well. It's harder to trust someone we can't see than someone we can, but that is what Jesus asks us to do. In this session, we will stand with the disciples as Jesus gives them some words of encouragement about trusting His spiritual Presence.

1. *What is one specific thing that God has revealed to you during this study of His Presence? How are you grateful for that?*

2. *What's your immediate reaction when you contemplate the idea of helping others experience Jesus' presence? Does that excite you? Does it seem like one more burden or demand in an already burdened life? Are you still occupied with coming to rely on Jesus' Presence, or are you ready to move toward helping other people know Him like this more?*

EXPERIENCE IT

"Do not be discouraged by the difficulty of keeping your focus on Me. I know that your heart's desire is to be aware of My Presence continually. This is a lofty goal; you aim toward it but never fully achieve it in this life. Don't let feelings of failure weigh you down. Instead, try to see yourself as I see you. First of all, I am delighted by your deep desire to walk closely with Me through your life. I am pleased each time you initiate communication with Me. In addition, I notice the progress you have made since you first resolved to live in My Presence.

"When you realize that your mind has wandered away from Me, don't be alarmed or surprised. You live in a world that has been rigged to distract you. Each time you plow your way through the massive distractions to communicate with Me, you achieve a victory. Rejoice in these tiny triumphs, and they will increasingly light up your days."

—FROM *JESUS CALLING*, NOVEMBER 1

3. *How do you react when you find it hard to stay focused on Jesus' Presence? Do you have feelings of failure or surprise? Do you rejoice in tiny triumphs? Do you gently turn back to Jesus' Presence, or do you have to deal with guilt or other obstacles?*

4. *What are the things that make you aware that you live in a world that has been rigged to distract you from Jesus' Presence? How do you deal with those things?*

"Look to Me continually for help, comfort, and companionship. Because I am always by your side, the briefest glance can connect you with Me. When you look to Me for help, it flows freely from My Presence. This recognition of your need for Me, in small matters as well as in large ones, keeps you spiritually alive.

"When you need comfort, I love to enfold you in My arms. I enable you not only to feel comforted but also to be a channel through whom I comfort others. Thus you are doubly blessed, because a living channel absorbs some of whatever flows through it.

"My constant Companionship is the *pièce de résistance*: the summit of salvation blessings. No matter what losses you experience in your life, no one can take away this glorious gift."

—From *Jesus Calling*, October 16

5. *Do you find that Jesus' help flows freely to you from His Presence? If so, how do you experience that help? If not, what do you think gets in the way?*

6. *Are you in any way a vessel through whom Jesus comforts others? If you're meeting with a group, talk about ways the members in your group have helped you experience Jesus' comfort.*

STUDY IT

In this section, you'll reflect on a passage in which Jesus appears to His eleven disciples after His resurrection. He is getting ready to stop appearing to them in bodily form, and soon He will send the Holy Spirit to live inside them. He is preparing them for that transition from His physical Presence to His Presence in the Spirit. He is also preparing them for the work He will give them.

7. *Read the following passage aloud. Then spend several minutes in silence rereading the passage and picturing yourself in the scene, perhaps as one of the disciples (The group leader will need to keep track of time.)*

> Then the eleven disciples went to Galilee, to the mountain where Jesus had told them to go. When they saw him, they worshiped him; but some doubted. Then Jesus came to them and said, "All authority in heaven and on earth has been given to me. Therefore go and make disciples of all nations, baptizing them in the name of the Father and of the Son and of the Holy Spirit, and teaching them to obey everything I have commanded you. And surely I am with you always, to the very end of the age."
>
> —MATTHEW 28:16–20

Ask God to guide you, and use your senses to imagine the scene. What does Jesus look like in His resurrected body? What are His tone of voice and body language? What body language do you see in the disciples around you? How can you tell that some are worshiping and some are doubting? What do you feel as the scene unfolds? Write down notes about what you have recognized through this exercise.

8. *If you're meeting with a group, share your experience of putting yourself into this story. What was it like to imagine yourself with Jesus, receiving these instructions? Were you one of those who worshiped with wholehearted faith or one who doubted? How did Jesus' words affect you?*

9. *Why do you suppose Matthew makes a point of telling us that some of the disciples doubted Jesus?*

10. *What role might you have in Jesus' command to go and make disciples, baptizing them, and teaching them to obey Him? This is a command to the whole people of God, so it's not all on your shoulders alone, but you are a follower of Christ, you are a participant. What might your part be?*

11. *Are you in a season of life right now when being sent by Jesus feels like too much? Or are you in a season when you are ready to go into all the world and make disciples for Him? Does Jesus' promise to be with you in this work help you take it on with joy, or are you still not ready? Talk about the place you're in right now.*

12. *What might Jesus be saying to you through this Scripture passage?*

13. *If you're meeting with a group, how can the members pray for you? If you're using this study on your own, what would you like to say to God right now?*

LIVE IT

The theme of this week's readings is gently dealing with the possibility that Jesus wants you to reflect the light of His presence to others. Each day, read the passage slowly, pausing to think about what is being said. Remember that this is an opportunity to meet with a Person. Use any of the questions that are helpful.

Day 1

Read John 15:1–5. How important is it for a branch to bear fruit?

How does a branch bear fruit?

What does it mean to remain conected to Jesus?

How do you cultivate that connection?

Talk with Jesus about your connection and the fruit He wants to produce from it.

Day 2

Reread John 15:1–5 and then read 15:12–13. What is the fruit that will come from a connection to Jesus?

What effort does that fruit require from us? What effort does it require from Jesus?

As a believer, do you ever have feelings of failure about not bearing enough fruit? What do you think Jesus thinks about those feelings? Does He see you as a failure, or does He celebrate what He's doing in you?

Day 3

Read John 17:13–24. This is part of a long prayer Jesus is praying to the Father for His disciples. What does He ask for?

Go through each request and pray for the Father to do this for you. Which requests stand out to you as most important for you right now?

*Note that to **sanctify** something is to set it apart for God's holy use. Why does Jesus ask that His followers be truly set apart like this?*

_____

_____

_____

_____

Why is oneness among God's people so important to the Lord? What does such unity communicate to the world?

_____

_____

_____

_____

Day 4

Read John 20:19–23. "Peace be with you" was a standard greeting, but Jesus repeats it. How did it have special meaning in this situation, Jesus' first appearance to His male disciples after His resurrection?

_____

_____

_____

_____

What did the Father send Jesus to do? What does Jesus send His disciples to do?

Why was the Holy Spirit necessary for this?

What does forgiveness have to do with it? How might the ministry of forgiveness be part of what Jesus sends you to do?

Day 5

Read Matthew 5:14–16. How is it possible to be the light of the world?

As a believer, is this something you can do simply by trying hard? Where does the light come from?

What actions are the equivalent of hiding your light under a bowl? What actions make the light in you available to others?

Ask God today to help you to do these things.

LEADER'S NOTES

Thank you for your willingness to lead a group through this *Jesus Calling* study. The rewards of being a leader are different from the rewards of participating, and we hope you find your own walk with Jesus deepened by this experience. In many ways, your group meeting will be structured like other Bible studies in which you've participated. You'll want to open in prayer, for example, and ask people to silence their phones. These leader's notes will focus on elements of the study that may be new to you.

CONSIDER IT

This first portion of the study functions as an icebreaker. It gets the group members thinking about the topic at hand by asking them to share things from their experience. Some people may want to tell a long story in response to one of these questions, but the goal is to keep answers brief. Ideally, you want everyone in the group to get a chance to respond to the *Consider It* questions, so you may want to explain up front that everyone needs to limit his or her answer to one minute.

With the rest of the study, it's generally not a good idea to have everyone answer every question—a free-flowing discussion is more desirable. But with the *Consider It* questions, you can go around the circle. Encourage shy people to share, but don't force them. Tell the group members they should feel free to pass if they prefer not to answer one of these questions.

EXPERIENCE IT

This is the group's chance to talk about excerpts from the *Jesus Calling* devotional. You will need to monitor this discussion closely so that you have enough time for the Bible study. If the group has a long and rich discussion on one of the devotional excerpts, you may choose to skip the other one and move on to the Bible study. Don't feel obliged to cover every question if the discussion is fruitful. On the other hand, do move on if the group starts to ramble or gets off on a tangent.

STUDY IT

Try to do the *Study It* exercise in session 1 on your own before the group meets the first time so that you can coach people on what to expect. Note that this section may be a little different from Bible studies you and the group members have done in the past. The group will spend five to ten minutes in silence, praying through the Scripture passage. It will be up to you to keep track of the time and call people back to the discussion when the time is up. (There are some good phone apps for timers that play a gentle chime or other pleasant sound instead of a disruptive noise.) If this is the group's first time doing an exercise like this, five minutes of silence may feel like plenty. By the time you get to sessions 5 and 6, they may be ready for ten minutes. Use your judgment based on feedback you get.

Don't be afraid to let people sit in silence. Group members can sit where they are in the circle, or if you have space, you can let them go off alone to another room. As you introduce the exercise, tell them where they are free to go. If your group meets in a home, ask the host before the meeting which rooms are available for use. Some people will be more comfortable in silence if they have a bit of space from others.

When the group gathers back together after the time of silence, invite them to share what they experienced. There are several questions provided in this study guide that you can ask. Note that it's not necessary to cover every question if the group has a good discussion going. Again, it's also not necessary to go around the circle and make everyone share.

Don't be concerned if the group members are quiet after the exercise and slow to share. People are often quiet when they are pulling together their ideas, and the exercise will have been a new experience for many of them. Just ask a question and let it hang in the air until someone shares. You can then say, "Thank you. What about others? What came to you when you sat with the passage?"

Some people may say they found it hard to quiet their minds enough to focus on the passage for several minutes. Tell them that's okay. They are practicing a skill, and sometimes skills take time to learn. If they learn to sit quietly with God's Word in a group, they will become much more comfortable sitting with the Word on their own.

Remind them that spending time each day in God's Word is one of the most valuable things they can do for their spiritual lives. Also, imagining the Bible passage isn't the one right way to spend time with God. Analytical Bible study is also good, and they will be doing some of that in their daily Bible readings. This study simply exposes them to an approach they may want to add to their menu of ways to spend time with God in His Word.

One concern some people may have with picturing themselves in the passage is it requires them to "add" things to the text that aren't there. That's an important concern, but it shouldn't be taken to extremes. Whenever we read a story in the Bible, we have to imagine it to some degree in order to understand it. The question is whether we imagine it deeply or shallowly, deliberately or carelessly.

For instance, whenever we see someone speaking in the Bible, we need to deeply and deliberately imagine the tone of voice and body language with which the words are spoken. Is the speaker angry, afraid, joking? If the characters are on a boat in a storm, we need to imagine what it's like to be on a boat in a storm, or the story has no impact. Of course, our depiction of things like a character's tone of voice needs to be held lightly, because we could be wrong. But trying on the possibilities is something we're meant to do when exploring the text.

PREPARATION

It's not necessary for group members to prepare anything for the study ahead of time. At the end of each study are suggestions for ways they can spend time in God's Word during the next five days of the week. These daily times are optional but valuable, so encourage the group to do them. Also invite them to bring their questions and insights back to the group at your next meeting, especially if they had a breakthrough moment or if they didn't understand something.

As the leader, there are a few things you should do to prepare for each meeting:

- *Read through the session.* This will help you to become familiar with the content and know how to structure the discussion times.

- *Spend five to ten minutes doing the Bible reflection exercise on your own.* When the group meets, you'll be watching the clock, so you'll probably have a more fulfilling time with the passage if you do the exercise ahead of time. You can then reread the passage again when the group meets. This way, you'll be sure to have the passage even more deeply in your mind than group members do.

- *Pray for your group.* Pray especially that God will guide them into a greater experience of His presence.

- *Bring extra supplies to your meeting.* Group members should bring their own pens for writing notes, but it is a good idea to have extras available for those who forget. You may also want to bring paper and additional Bibles for those who forget to bring their study guides.

Below you will find suggested answers for some of the study questions. Note that in many cases there is no one right answer. Answers will vary, especially when the group members are sharing their personal experiences.

Session 1: God's Presence Invites You

1. *This question is an invitation for group members to share their experience and beliefs about God's Presence. If anyone in the group expresses skepticism, simply thank him or her for being honest—it's not necessary to try to convince the person otherwise. If you have time, though, do ask the individual to share the reason for his or her belief. For those group members who aren't sure whether God wants them to experience His Presence when they read the Scriptures, the best persuasion will be getting into the Bible and seeing what happens. Not everyone will feel dramatic emotions—God's Presence comes to people differently.*

2. *Give everyone a chance to share, but let them pass if they prefer.*

3. *Most people who join a study group want to experience change, but not everyone does. It's good to be aware of each person's openness to change.*

4. *Possible answers include fear of the new or the unknown, fear of failure, not wanting to do the work that change requires, preferring what is familiar, and being unsure of how loved ones will react. It's completely understandable to find change uncomfortable.*

5. *Most people want God to be more attentive than they feel He is, but some are sensitive to how huge, powerful, and different He is from us. It's not at all bad to be aware of the holiness of God.*

6. *Spending time in God's Presence renews, relaxes, and refocuses His children when they're drained or stressed. It equips believers to deal with whatever the day brings. It pleases God and strengthens those who walk with Him, helping them reaffirm the priorities He has given them.*

7. *Answers will vary. Encourage group members to think deeply about how they really believe God sees them. Many of us doubt God's delight in us, especially because we tend to base it on our performance rather than His unchanging nature.*

8. *The renewing of one's mind is a transformation not just of what a person thinks but of how he or she sees God, other people, and the world. It is a change in the Christian's spiritual lens—a redirecting of one's mind so that it takes a different direction when it is idle or stressed or drained.*

9. *Review the instructions carefully, and make sure everyone understands them. Then tell the group how much time they have on their own to put themselves in the passage (allow five to ten minutes). Suggest where in your meeting space group members can go if there is more than one room available, then break for this exercise, and keep track of the time. You may find that some people want more time. Use your discretion.*

10. *Answers will vary. It's fine for this process to be unfamiliar at first.*

11. *Answers will vary. In later sessions there will be some more focused questions for discussing the passage, but in this first session the questions are wide open to whatever people experienced. The goal is to learn to do what Mary did: to sit at Jesus' feet and learn from Him. But it is equally fruitful for participants to imagine themselves in Martha's place as the doer who is frustrated by the one who merely sits. We all need some Mary and some Martha in our lives, with a balance that is unique to each of us.*

12. *Answers will vary.*

13. *Take as much time as you can to pray for each other. You might have someone write down the prayer requests so that you can keep track of answers to prayer.*

Session 2: God's Presence Restores You

1. *You may need to ask people to keep their answers brief, as some may want to talk at length about their families. The goal here is to recognize that our pressure to perform often comes from the people in our childhood, not from God.*

2. *This is as much a matter of personality as it is of spiritual maturity. Some people are just wired to be more self-scrutinizing than others. Some of us need to develop further awareness of our sin, while others of us need to learn to be more accepting of God's grace.*

3. *Many people feel that God views them much more harshly than He does. He knows we are made of dust. It's true that He is under no illusion about our sin, but if we have faith in Christ, He views us as clothed in Christ's righteousness.*

4. *Answers will vary. The Scriptures and the encouragement of other believers help. The voices of the world, the accusations of the enemy, and sometimes our own super-critical hearts can get in the way.*

5. *If any group members haven't received God's forgiveness, privately offer to sit down with them after the meeting and lead them in a prayer of repentance. If they're not ready to pray such a prayer, you can inquire about the things keeping them from taking that step. God is eager to forgive anyone who asks.*

6. *Answers will vary. Most of us naturally move away from God out of shame when we feel we aren't living up to His standards, but we need to cultivate the habit of moving toward Him at those times. He longs to take away our shame.*

7. *Answers will vary and may include reading the Bible, praying, reading a book that helps them in their spiritual walk, receiving encouragement from other people, listening to certain songs, and reviewing the biblical names of God.*

8. *Adjust the time allotted for this based on what happened in session 1.*

9. *Answers will vary. Hopefully the exercise will help deepen the group's sense of Jesus' Presence and widen their understanding of how it may affect a person.*

10. *When Jesus performed this miracle of the great catch of fish, Simon realized he was in the Presence of Someone much greater than himself, and the experience made him ashamed and conscious of his own sinfulness. Simon had previously recognized Jesus as "Master," but now he saw Christ as his Lord. In the same way, sometimes an experience of Jesus' greatness makes us conscious of our own smallness.*

11. *Jesus knew Simon's sinfulness completely; He wasn't shocked by it. He also didn't need Simon to wallow in shame and guilt. Once Simon was aware of his guilt, Jesus wanted to help him move past it into a new relationship with Him. Jesus had good plans for Simon.*

12. *Answers will vary.*

13. *Responses will vary.*

Session 3: God's Presence Strengthens You

1. *Answers will vary. The goal here is for people to be aware of what they do when they are desperate.*

2. *Answers may include trying to hide weakness; collapsing in weakness; numbing ourselves with food, TV, social media, work, or other distractions; talking with the Lord about it (which is a good way to deal with it), or talking to a friend (another positive response). Make your group a safe place for people to tell the truth about themselves. Establish confidentiality as a ground rule—whatever is shared in the group stays among you.*

3. *If we know that our weakness stirs God's compassion, we are more likely to move toward Him rather than away from Him in difficult times.*

4. *Answers will vary. Offer any help you can if someone is finding it hard to spend time in the Scriptures, and solicit input from other members of the group who may have struggled with the same issue. If necessary, you can talk further with that person after the meeting.*

5. *Answers will vary. Again, ensure that your group is a safe place for difficult stories. If someone needs more time than the meeting permits, offer to talk afterward.*

6. *It's okay for people to admit God seemed absent; this is a normal experience. Hopefully being in this group will give people the chance to have a different experience.*

7. *For the redeemed, some of the things that can get in the way are a lack of Bible training growing up, poor past Bible teaching, negative messages retained from childhood, legalistic thinking that creates difficulties in accepting God's grace, and disappointing experiences with the church. Pray that God will make your group a place where believers can learn to be treated as redeemed saints.*

8. *It may be helpful to go through the background information that precedes the question. Not everyone will necessarily be familiar with Hagar's story, and the passage you are going to read picks up in the middle of that story.*

9. *Answers will vary.*

10. *Group members shouldn't feel pressured to manufacture a sense of God's Presence. God will make Himself real in His own way to each individual.*

11. *Either opinion is possible. In either case, invite group members to explain the reason for their thinking. What God did was right (God is perfectly good), but it's understandable to want God to change our circumstances so we don't feel pain. God doesn't always do this, and He doesn't always tell us the reason. Nevertheless, we can know that He is good and that He intends the best for each person.*

12. *Answers will vary.*

13. *Responses will vary.*

Session 4: God's Presence Brings You Peace

1. *Answers will vary. The goal is for people to become aware of how they developed some of their fears and how they handle those fears today.*

2. *Answers will vary. Almost everyone is afraid of something.*

3. *Quality time with Jesus means spending enough time with Him—and time that is as free of external distractions as possible. People can aim for at least ten to fifteen minutes alone in a quiet place, but they should also be gracious to themselves! God knows if they have small children or other commitments they can't entirely escape, even briefly. The goal of this question should be to encourage each other, not to judge.*

4. *As the leader, you might want to try this idea of whispering Jesus' Name for at least a few days so that you can report to the group how it affected you.*

5. *God is delighted when we speak Jesus' Name in prayer and in ways that bring Him glory. This question is meant to motivate the group to actually try speaking Jesus' Name during the day.*

6. *Habit-blockers may include feeling embarrassed to do it at work or around nonbelievers, forgetfulness, busyness, and being accustomed to turning to our phones whenever we have a free moment.*

7. *Review the background information that precedes the question.*

8. *Answers will vary. Hopefully members will have a vivid mental picture of being in the boat. Perhaps the disciples shouted their words with wild gestures, and Jesus spoke quietly. We can't know each person's tone of voice for sure, but we are meant to think intentionally about how we envision the scene.*

9. *Since storms on the Sea of Galilee could be life-threatening, especially for men in a small fishing boat, their fears were reasonable from a human perspective. However, if the disciples had truly been confident in who Jesus was, they would have known they had nothing to fear with Him there.*

10. *Some people think the disciples' calling on Jesus for help was the right thing to do, but they should have done it without panicking. Others think they should have trusted Jesus and let Him sleep. Jesus said they had "little faith" because they didn't trust Him to be Master of the wind and waves.*

11. *Answers will vary. Great faith in the midst of the storms of life could take the form of asking God for help and completely trusting Him to provide the answer, or stepping out of our comfort zones to do what we feel God is asking us to do (even though it's difficult), or believing that God will carry us through the storm even though we can't see any possible way out.*

12. *Answers will vary.*

13. *Responses will vary.*

Session 5: God's Presence Awes You

1. *Answers will vary. The goal here is to see if the group members' past experiences have primed them to think negatively of awe (because they feared a harsh father, for example) or positively (because they had a kind father who was nonetheless much bigger and stronger than they were).*

2. *Awe involves a mix of emotions: dread, reverence, wonder, admiration. A healthy fear of God's power mixes with a healthy wonder at His grace and goodness. Encourage members to share times when they have felt such emotions.*

3. *Expect some members to feel positive toward God's might and glory, and some to feel unsettled by it. God wants us to be drawn to His overwhelming greatness, but He understands our limits as mere humans and that we can only absorb so much of His holiness. A negative experience with our earthly fathers or our drive to be in control at all times are two things that can make God's greatness feel uncomfortable.*

4. *This statement was coined by an ancient Greek philosopher. It means that each person is the judge (or measure) of how things are perceived, making the individual the measure of his or her own reality. By contrast, if God is the measure of all things, then He decides what is real, true, good, and beautiful. We need to try to see things as much as possible from His point of view.*

5. *Attuning to God in the Scriptures involves paying attention to His written Word, listening to the Holy Spirit, and trying to understand things from His point of view. It also means seeking to know what He requires of us and obeying Him.*

6. *Answers will vary. Encourage the group to continually seek God's Presence. Even small progress is worth celebrating!*

7. *Review the background information before the question. By this time the group is hopefully able to handle ten minutes of silence.*

8. *Isaiah's experience was somewhat like Simon Peter's: when faced with God's power and holiness, he felt fear and became aware of his sin. Isaiah's experience is perhaps even more frightening. God isn't tame, but He is good.*

9. *In Isaiah's day, people knew that seeing the Lord could kill a person, because a sinful person couldn't survive in the Presence of the holy God. In Exodus 33:20, when Moses asked to see God's glory, the Lord replied, "You cannot see my face, for no one may see me and live."*

10. *Unclean lips represented Isaiah's sinfulness. He was unclean (impure) in light of God's holiness, but he focused on his lips because he was painfully aware of the contrast between his worldly thoughts and the worshipful expressions of the seraphim. The coal from the altar of sacrifice purified his lips so that he could speak God's words as a prophet. In that day, the shedding of blood through an animal sacrifice pointed forward to the sacrifice of Christ, which truly purifies those who trust in Him so that those who believe in Him don't have to be terrified in the Presence of God.*

11. *See the answer to question 10. Because of Jesus' sacrifice, God is far more accessible to us. Our awe can have much less dread and more wonder. We don't need to fear dying when we see His holiness.*

12. *Answers will vary.*

13. *Responses will vary.*

Session 6: God's Presence Saves You

1. *Rather than telling the whole story of the loss, group members should focus on what they did to handle it. If someone's loss is current and they need a listening ear, you may want to spend time with them after the meeting.*

2. *Anger is the normal response. Some people lash back at the person who has treated them unfairly, others nurse anger inside, and others vent their feelings to a third party. Ideally, the goal is to develop the capacity to let go of our anger in forgiveness.*

3. *Viewing mistreatment as an opportunity for spiritual growth is often a difficult and unpleasant concept for us to accept. Yet the Bible clearly tells us that God allows trials into our lives to build up our faith. As James writes, "Consider it pure joy, my brothers and sisters, whenever you face trials of many kinds, because you know that the testing of your faith produces perseverance" (James 1:2–3).*

4. *Anything painful seems unfair. Losses that others haven't suffered may also seem unfair. Many people feel that God treats them less than fairly. This questions gives group members the opportunity to admit those feelings and to entertain the possibility that they are seeing things in a distorted way.*

5. *Some things that help are regular time alone with God, encouragement and support from other Christians, and time in worship. Some things that get in the way are mental patterns of fear and false beliefs about suffering, such as thinking that God is unjust and uncaring when He allows trials to come our way.*

6. *People often aren't aware of how constant busyness can unsettle their spirit and make them less attuned to God. The world seems so real, and God starts to feel unreal simply because they don't take time to be still with Him.*

7. *Read the background information that precedes the question.*

8. *Being with Jesus in His suffering is dramatically different from standing before the holy God in the temple with Isaiah. It's hard to imagine a majestic, holy God making Himself so vulnerable for our sake, but He did. It is hoped that this passage will deeply move your group members and motivate them to draw closer to God in trust. This is God being more than fair to us.*

9. *Answers will vary. Some might imagine that Jesus spoke with a quiet, rasping voice because He was thirsty and in terrible pain. They might imagine God speaking to Isaiah with a kingly, robust voice.*

10. *This would be the worst imaginable experience for a mother, and hanging on to faith would require a tremendous commitment. Yet Mary faced it bravely. We know her faith remained intact because, after Jesus' resurrection, she was with the disciples, waiting for the Holy Spirit (see Acts 1:12–14).*

11. *This returns to the subject of question 1, but now the group can view their losses through the lens of Jesus' and Mary's responses: the loss Jesus voluntarily suffered, and the grief Jesus' mother faithfully endured. Mary had good reason to feel that God was absent when her son hung on the cross. Encourage your group to talk about the experience of God's absence with a renewed sense that maybe He wasn't absent after all.*

12. *Answers will vary.*

13. *Responses will vary.*

Session 7: God's Presence Gives You Joy

1. *This is a chance to check in on how daily time with the Lord may have changed people's awareness of God's Presence. Celebrate with those who sense progress, and encourage those who feel that things haven't changed. Be sure that no one gives advice that isn't asked for.*

2. *Again, this is a chance to reinforce a habit that was introduced earlier in the study. Urge group members to try this again if they forgot about it.*

3. *Answers will vary, but most of us suffer at least occasionally from the stress of waiting for something we think should have already happened. Trusting in God and relying on the promises in His Word help us not run ahead of His timing, as does recalling His provision and protection in times past.*

4. *Life might not be a bed of roses, but if a person practices this as a habit, he or she often experiences less anxiety and a greater capacity to deal with whatever life delivers.*

5. *We've seen Isaiah and Simon Peter being terrified at the closeness of the Holy One whom they were not worthy to approach. Because of Jesus' sacrifice, Christians no longer need to be terrified of God's holiness—awe and respect and reverence are always in order, but not dread. For those who haven't accepted Jesus' sacrifice, they may feel the terror, especially if they hate letting go of control. God is indeed uncontrollable.*

6. *Answers will vary.*

7. *Review the background information that precedes the question.*

8. *Answers will vary.*

9. *We don't know for sure. In some instances, those who knew Jesus personally before His resurrection didn't immediately recognize Him (see Luke 24:13–35), while in other instances His friends and family did know who He was (see Matthew 28:8–10; Luke 24:36–43; John 20:26–28). Perhaps in this case Jesus looked different—with a body that didn't show the signs of torture or earthly wear and tear. He may have looked younger and healthier. There may have been other differences as well that we can only guess at. In part, He didn't always choose to be recognized at first.*

10. *Answers will vary. Mary was probably expressing her profound love for Jesus, her relief, and her utter astonishment. Perhaps Jesus spoke her name softly and with affection.*

11. *Jesus was preparing Mary for a change in their relationship. He wouldn't be physically available forever. She was now a witness to His resurrection, and He was sending her out to share with others the truth of what she had witnessed.*

12. *Answers will vary.*

13. *Responses will vary.*

Session 8: God's Presence Empowers You

1. *Answers will vary. This is a chance for group members to look back and celebrate the good, to bring closure to the group experience.*

2. *Some within the group will be in hard places, and they will need more time to rest in Jesus' Presence without being asked to do anything. Others will be ready to pay forward what they have received. Affirm wherever they are on their journey of faith.*

3. *Answers will vary. Encourage those who default toward negative attitudes to be honest about how they feel, and urge the group not to pressure them to be different. Offer them the gift of being heard.*

4. *That we live in such a media-driven and convenience-driven world is one reason we may find it hard to focus on Jesus' Presence. We have an abundance of distractions today, and it is easy to fall into the mind-set that everything should come quickly and easily to us.*

5. *Busyness and unbelief are two big obstacles that get in the way of our experiencing Jesus' Presence.*

6. *Allow group members this opportunity to express gratitude to each other. If some in the group get thanked, but not every person, find ways to affirm the contributions and efforts of each of the others as well.*

7. *Review the background information that precedes the question.*

8. *Answers will vary.*

9. *We don't know for sure, but Matthew seems to want us to know that it wasn't easy for some of the disciples to believe that Jesus was the divine Son of God who deserved their worship. For a Jew, worship was given to God alone—so to worship Jesus would be to acknowledge that He was and is God. Also, those who were clear on Jesus' identity may have been uncertain about the implications. What should they do now? They weren't used to serving Him without having Him bodily present. Matthew allows us to admit our doubts even as we commit to worshiping and following Jesus.*

10. *Answers will vary. Be careful that this question doesn't come across as pressuring people to do what they're not ready for. God invites them to participate in the great work He is doing in the world.*

11. *Answers will vary. Affirm the place where each person is currently.*

12. *Answers will vary.*

13. *Responses will vary.*

ENJOY JESUS' PRESENCE.
FIND COMFORT
IN HIS PEACE.

Selected quotes and scriptures from **Jesus Calling**
along with inspiring images will encourage you to
worship and find comfort in the peace of the Lord.

www.jesuscalling.com